PEVENSEY C

EAST SUSSEX

John Goodall, PhD

Pevensey Castle has a history stretching back over 1,700 years. Originally a Roman fort, it was refortified by the Normans after William the Conqueror landed at Pevensey in 1066 and a great medieval castle was subsequently built within the Roman walls. This fell into decay in the late Middle Ages, but its defences have twice been renewed: once to protect England from the Spanish Armada in 1588, and again during the Second World War.

This guidebook offers a brief tour of the medieval and Roman buildings at Pevensey, as well as a short history of the castle.

❖ CONTENTS ❖

Acknowledgements

Thanks to: Kevin Booth, Michael Fulford,
Jonathan Coad.

Published by English Heritage
1 Waterhouse Square, 138–142 Holborn, London EC1N 2ST
© English Heritage 1999
First published by English Heritage 1999
Reprinted 2004, 2006, 2007, 2008, 2013
Revised reprint 2011, 2016
Photographs, unless otherwise specified, were taken by English Heritage Photographic Unit
and remain the copyright of English Heritage (Photographic library tel. 01793 414903)

Edited by Lorimer Poultney
Designed by Derek Lee
Plans by Hardlines; illustration on p. 10 by Ray Martin Art Services
Printed in England by Park Communications Ltd
C45 08/16 06693 ISBN 978 1 85074 722 2

INTRODUCTION

❖

Pevensey Castle is one of Britain's oldest and most important strongholds. Its impressive ruins stand on what was once a peninsula surrounded by sea and salt marsh projecting from the mainland of the Sussex coast. This naturally defensible site, commanding the Bay of Pevensey with its harbour, was first fortified in about AD 290 when a Roman fort called Anderida was built here. After the end of Roman rule in Britain, Anderida's walls continued to shelter a settlement until the late fifth century and possibly beyond. In 1066, the ruinous Roman defences were refortified by William the Conqueror, and a great castle subsequently developed here. Since its abandonment and decay in the early sixteenth century, the castle's walls have twice been remanned in response to a threatened invasion. A gun battery was erected here at the time of the Spanish Armada, and during the Second World War machine-gun posts and billets for troops were created within the ancient fabric of the buildings.

Aerial view of the castle. The medieval inner bailey occupies the bottom corner of the large Roman enclosure

TOUR AND DESCRIPTION

THE DEVELOPMENT OF THE CASTLE

The fortifications that survive at Pevensey Castle belong to three distinct periods: Roman, medieval and Second World War. Despite the changing needs of warfare, and the complete abandonment of the site between each period of occupation, every subsequent rebuilding has been influenced by the existing arrangement of the ruined defences.

Throughout its long history the most important line of defence has been the Roman fort wall. This encircles the high ground at what was the seaward tip of the peninsula. Incredibly, after 1,700 years two-thirds of its circuit still stands to virtually full height. In the Middle Ages it served as the outer perimeter of the castle, while the interior of the Roman fort was divided into two enclosures known as the inner and outer baileys.

The inner bailey was the heart of the medieval castle and contained all its principal domestic buildings including the great hall and the lord's lodgings. In the outer bailey were the secondary buildings, such as the granary for Pevensey manor.

When the castle was refortified in the Second World War advantage was once again taken of the high ground enclosed by the Roman fort and pillboxes were set around it. Several were built into the medieval ruins for added height, camouflage and protection and the garrison was billeted in the thirteenth-century towers of the inner bailey.

This guide will look at the remains of the medieval castle and then those of the Roman fort.

THE MEDIEVAL CASTLE

*The tour starts from in front of the great
gatehouse. Go back to the head of the
wooden bridge you crossed to enter the
inner bailey.*

Inner Bailey

You are standing at the main gateway
to the fortified enclosure, known as
the inner bailey, which was created in
the Middle Ages within the walls of
the Roman fort. This bailey changed
considerably in character over the
course of the castle's history and now
occupies a much smaller area than it
did when it was first created by the
Normans in the twelfth century.

Evidence of this larger Norman
bailey is still visible. If you look to
your left (northwards) you can see a
tower projecting above the line of the
Roman wall and, running towards
you in the grass beneath it, a slight
depression. This depression is
thought to mark the line of a ditch in
front of the timber defences of the
original inner bailey. When it was first
dug, this ditch would have extended
right across the Roman fort enclosure
and partitioned off its whole
north-eastern end. Behind the ditch
was an earth bank topped by a timber
palisade that would have joined with
the Roman fort wall at the point
where the projecting tower stands.
The upper sections of the tower –
which now contain a 1940s machine-
gun post – are medieval, and it
therefore seems likely that they were

*The inner bailey with its
gatehouse (to the left) viewed
from the medieval shoreline*

built as part of the Norman inner bailey defences.

In the mid-thirteenth century this inner bailey enclosure was roughly halved in size to create the present layout. Around it a vast new moat was dug. Parts of this have been re-excavated to create the ditch and pools you now see. These give little sense of the original's massive scale: the moat was probably more than 60 feet (18m) wide and the water in it would have lapped the bases of the walls and towers. A dam retained the water and the remains of this are visible in the ditch to your right (southwards).

Gatehouse

The gatehouse in front of you was probably built in about 1200 along the line of the Norman timber palisade to the inner bailey. It was incorporated within the new defences when the bailey was reduced to its present size in the mid-thirteenth century, and there is an untidy join between the masonry of the walls and gatehouse visible on both sides. The original approach to the gatehouse was across a massive 68 feet (20.7m) long wooden bridge, but this proved very expensive to maintain, and in 1405 the existing stone causeway and drawbridge pit were built to reduce its span.

The gatehouse had two great drum-shaped towers flanking the vaulted entrance passage – one of the earliest surviving examples of this popular medieval twin-towered design. Only one of these towers still stands but it is still possible to reconstruct something of the original architecture. The window-like openings in it mark the position of arrowslits. There were originally three tiers of these in each tower, and they have been widened by stone robbing. Only two, on the north face, survive in their original form. At the front of the entrance passage you

The gatehouse to the inner bailey was probably built in about 1200. The causeway and drawbridge pit in front of it are later medieval additions

can see a vertical groove in the masonry to your left (the north side). This is the chase for the portcullis.

On either side of the entrance passage there is a door opening into the interior of the gatehouse. Internally, the tower chambers on each of the three floors were D-shaped in plan and their open backs appear to have been closed by a wooden wall. The basement rooms of both towers have survived intact. That to the south can be entered down a spiral stair, but that to the north is only accessible through a hole in the roof and may have served as a prison cell. This is sometimes termed an 'oubliette'.

Keep

Dominating the eastern side of the inner bailey, and facing you as you enter it, is the ruin of the keep. This was once a great tower containing domestic apartments. Little of this once grand building survives today: its most imposing features are the bases of two towers that project towards the gatehouse and seem consciously to echo its twin-towered architectural design.

Until the early twentieth century the entire ruin was buried beneath a massive mound of earth and rubble, and the exposed remains you see today pose an architectural puzzle which still remains to be solved.

Looking across the inner bailey towards the keep. The foundations of the chapel are visible in the foreground

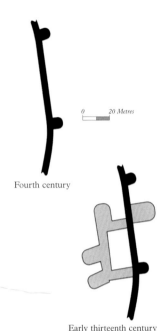

0 ___ 20 Metres

Fourth century

Early thirteenth century

c.1325

■ Roman
▨ Medieval keep
▨ Medieval rebuilding I
▨ Medieval rebuilding II

The development of the keep

In plan, the building latterly seems to have consisted of a central rectangular block, probably several storeys high, with seven projecting towers. This bizarre design is unique among medieval keeps and it is difficult to imagine what this building originally looked like or how it was arranged internally. Suggesting answers to these questions is made more complicated by the very fragmentary remains – only sections of the ground floor survive – and by the alterations made to its fabric during the Middle Ages.

As first constructed, the keep was built up against the Roman fort wall and incorporated a stretch of it, complete with one mural tower, as the lower stage of its eastern side. Four more towers were built against the rectangular core of the building: one to the north, one to the east against the Roman wall (now entirely lost) and two to the west. The date of this building work is uncertain. Some authorities have dated it as early as 1130, when documents refer to a 'tower' or keep at Pevensey. Although the keep could be the tower mentioned in 1130, it could equally be a later building altogether and the style of the masonry has been compared to that of the gatehouse, constructed in about 1200.

Whatever its date, the keep was radically altered in about 1325, when the medieval eastern tower, along with a substantial section of the

adjacent Roman wall, was thrown down and replaced by two new towers; construction work which must have entailed demolishing much of the upper part of the building. At the same time, a skin of medieval masonry was built along the remaining length of the keep's Roman east wall. Slightly later, but in conjunction with these repairs, a rectangular tower of masonry was constructed up against the building's south-west corner. This has been dubiously identified by some scholars as a catapult tower and by others as a forebuilding, or tower entrance, to the keep. When this was done the base of the remaining Roman tower on the keep's eastern side was ringed with stone. Quite why these alterations were made is a matter of speculation. One plausible explanation is that the keep suffered a major structural failure, possibly as the result of siege damage, and had to be shored up in some way.

Little of architectural interest survives in the standing medieval fabric, while the construction of a Second World War machine-gun post has obscured much of the upper structure. One feature to note is the way in which the exposed rubble core of the keep seems to shelve away in steps. These mark the regular 'lifts' or layers in which the building was raised, stage by stage, during its construction.

The internal layout of the keep is now impossible to reconstruct but fourteenth-century documents describe it as containing a kitchen and a chapel. Its main entrance was closed with an iron door and was approached up a wooden stair.

For most of the fourteenth century the building was in a dilapidated condition and regularly underwent extensive, and apparently ineffective, repair.

Postern

In the stretch of Roman wall to the right (south) of the keep there is a twelfth-century postern – a side-gate for direct external access. The gate opened onto a platform created by a collapsed Roman tower and its door was secured by a heavy wooden bar. One of the deep, square sockets in the masonry which secured this is still visible on one side of the door opening.

Curtain Wall

The curtain wall that divides the inner bailey from the Roman fort enclosure was built by Peter of Savoy after he was granted the castle by Henry III in 1246. It was originally

The postern gate, seen from inside the castle. This gave access to the medieval shore

❖ THE FIREPLACES OF THE BAILEY BUILDINGS ❖

The backs of the fireplaces which warmed the buildings within the inner bailey are visible at regular intervals along the wall. Large projecting hoods of lath and timber would have completed their design.

Although the size of the fireplaces would suggest that they heated substantial rooms, in some places, notably on the east side adjacent to the keep, these buildings must actually have been very narrow.

The back of one of the fireplaces that can be seen built into the curtain wall. This one is in the south curtain wall.

Conjectural reconstruction of one of the fireplaces

crowned by a crenellated parapet and lined along the interior with domestic buildings. These were timber-framed and several of the most substantial, such as the great hall and its chamber, are named in building accounts of the thirteenth and fourteenth centuries.

Their precise arrangement is not known and the most important appear to have been totally rebuilt on at least one occasion, by Edward I in 1301–2.

Begin to walk clockwise round the inner bailey.

East, North and South Curtain Towers

The three great towers of the inner bailey are contemporary with Peter of Savoy's curtain wall, built after 1246. Their masonry is of very high quality and all follow a similar and unusual design, with three floors reached separately: access to the basement is down a flight of steps built back into the bailey under a porch; the ground floor along a short passage; and the upper floor through a doorway opening onto a platform at wall-walk level (probably reached by a wooden stair). The rooms inside are lit by arrowslits, and the upper room in each probably served as a lodging and was heated by a fireplace. Each tower is also flanked by a doorway and latrine punched through the adjacent curtain wall on either side. These are entered respectively from the stair and ground-floor passage.

Curiously, the South and West Towers were left uncompleted until at least 1317, when an estimate was drawn up for providing the otherwise finished structures with castellations and proper lead roofs, rather than thatching. Whether this work was actually carried out is not known. These two towers were both refitted in 1940 to create barracks but the North Tower's medieval interior is still well preserved. Particularly noteworthy is the basement, which is unique among the towers for being vaulted with stone, possibly because it was the only one that was ever finished. Sadly the vault was largely destroyed when, after a period of neglect before 1317, the rotten roof and floors of the tower above collapsed through it. The North Tower contains an exhibition on the history of the castle.

When you climb the stairs to the upper chambers of the North Tower, look along the top of the adjacent curtain walls. Notice how the chimneys from the fireplaces of the bailey buildings blocked the wall-walks. To walk along these it must have therefore been necessary to cross over the roof.

Looking along the present-day coastline from this vantage-point it is possible to see some Martello towers, a line of Napoleonic gun-forts built to defend Britain against possible French invasion.

The North Tower before the alterations carried out during the Second World War

The East Tower, seen from the level of the wall-walk of the curtain wall

❖ THE PEVENSEY CANNON ❖

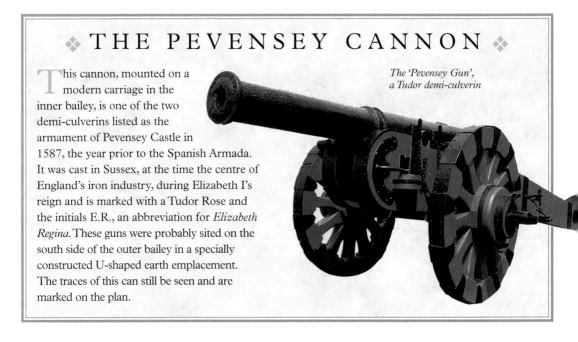

This cannon, mounted on a modern carriage in the inner bailey, is one of the two demi-culverins listed as the armament of Pevensey Castle in 1587, the year prior to the Spanish Armada. It was cast in Sussex, at the time the centre of England's iron industry, during Elizabeth I's reign and is marked with a Tudor Rose and the initials E.R., an abbreviation for *Elizabeth Regina*. These guns were probably sited on the south side of the outer bailey in a specially constructed U-shaped earth emplacement. The traces of this can still be seen and are marked on the plan.

*The 'Pevensey Gun',
a Tudor demi-culverin*

Chapel

In the middle of the inner bailey lawn are the outlines of stone foundations belonging to a chapel. This chapel's existence is documented by the thirteenth century, when it stood in a little enclosure surrounded by palings. It was entirely rebuilt in wood in 1302, either on this foundation or on a new site in the outer bailey.

The Well

Beside the chapel is a well. The shaft is lined with stone to a depth of over 50 feet (15m) and with wood beyond that. It has never been fully dug out.

THE ROMAN FORT

When you have finished looking at the inner bailey buildings walk back out through the gatehouse and continue straight down the hill to the Roman West Gate. To your left (east) you pass the earthworks of the former Elizabethan gun battery.

Anderida, the Roman fort at Pevensey, was built in about AD 290. It is one of the largest Roman forts to survive in Britain and its massive walls and towers still stand to virtually their full height around most of the 10-acre site they encircle. The irregular oval plan of the defences is unique among contemporary Roman forts (which are normally rectangular or square) and was determined by the shape of the high ground of the Pevensey peninsula. Because the fort was naturally protected by marsh or sea to both the north and south, the towers which strengthen the perimeter are grouped together at the more exposed eastern and western extremes of the circuit. Projecting D-shaped towers of this kind are a feature of late Roman military architecture and probably served to mount *ballistae* – catapults and heavy crossbows. At opposite ends of the fort, set amid these clusters of towers, are the two main entrances.

West Gate

The West Gate was the principal entrance to the fort and faced the narrow causeway that formerly connected Pevensey to the mainland. It is set between two wall towers and was originally approached across a ditch which bisected the causeway. The gateway itself was a narrow arched passageway set in the gorge behind the towers and the rectangular foundations of the buildings to either side of the passageway are marked in the ground. There was a very similar gateway arrangement at the late third-century Roman fort of Portchester.

A view northwards along the Roman wall to the left of the West Gate, showing two D-shaped bastions. In typical Roman fashion the walls were faced with small blocks of squared stone and strengthened by so-called bonding courses of brick

During the Middle Ages a new gatehouse was constructed on the site of the Roman one. All that remains of this medieval work are a few stones of its western gatepost. There was also a medieval defensive ditch cut across the causeway at a different angle to the Roman one.

The Exterior of the Fort

Walk through the gate and along the exterior of the wall to your right (west).

From outside the gate it is possible to gain an impression of the massive scale of the Roman walls and towers, the largest of any surviving contemporary fort. Externally they stand up to 30 feet (9m) high and are faced with dark-coloured ironstone and a lighter green sandstone. Courses of brick in two sizes run through the wall. In some places the remains of crenellations are visible along the top of the wall. These are probably medieval but they are likely to have replaced similar Roman ones.

Go back through the West Gate into the fort.

The Interior of the Fort

We know very little about how the interior of the Roman fort was arranged, and excavations have so far failed to reveal any significant

The Roman West Gate. The gate passage was in a building set between these two towers. The walls and gateway of the inner bailey are visible in the distance

BARRY CUNLIFFE

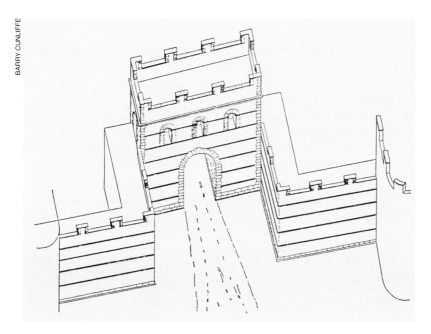

Reconstruction drawing of the late third-century Landgate at Porchester Castle as it may have appeared in Roman times. The West Gate at Pevensey followed a similar design with a rectangular gatehouse set between two drum towers

buildings within it. A series of regularly placed Roman hearths were excavated near the centre of the enclosure and these may have belonged to a series of symmetrically arranged wooden barrack blocks.

Follow the Roman wall round to your left (northwards) up to the point where it has fallen away.

Postern Gate

Passing through the wall at the point where it has collapsed are the remains of a small Roman side gate, or 'postern'. It takes the form of a curved passageway. The damage to the masonry around it shows the careful manner in which the wall was

built. All the outer surfaces of the wall have a fine pink mortar cementing the masonry, but in the core a rougher white mortar has been used.

Walk northwards past the collapsed section of the Roman wall until you come to the standing fabric again.

The Roman Wall

You can see the structure of the Roman wall most clearly in this area where, during an archaeological excavation, the earth was dug away down to the foundations. The wall is about 12 feet (3.7m) thick and faced on both sides with small blocks of finely cut stone. It was built in sections and in some places along the outer face of the wall you can see the vertical breaks in the masonry which mark the extent of these. These building breaks should not be confused with the many irregular vertical fissures in the wall which have been caused by weathering and uneven structural settlement. Internally the Roman ground level was probably artificially raised to the level of the projecting step in the back of the wall, a point much higher than on the exterior.

Excavation has revealed that the wall is supported below ground by a complex timber and rubble foundation. To create this, a ditch 15 feet (4.6m) deep was dug and the earth from it cast inside the fort. Piles made of oak trunks were then driven into the bottom of the trench and a layer of flint and clay packed around them. Above this, and set in a thick layer of flint and chalk, was a horizontal criss-cross frame of oak beams. Where there are projecting

A reconstruction drawing by Peter Dunn of the Roman fort at Portchester, built about the same time as Pevensey, showing how the Roman wall was built in sections by gangs of soldiers. It was erected on a timber and rubble foundation sealed with cement

The East Gate from the inside of the fort. The road, which formerly ran through the fort, is now diverted around it

towers the framework was extended into the tower. This whole foundation was then sealed by a thin layer of cement and this has preserved the imprint of the long-rotted oak frame it covered. Some of the oak piles have, however, survived and been exposed. Their dendrochronological (tree-ring) dating suggests that the fort was built in the late third century.

Continue northwards round the fort perimeter, crossing over the line of the Norman inner bailey, and pass through the East Gate.

East Gate

The plain archway of the Roman East Gate probably appears much as it did in Roman times, although it has been rebuilt both in the Middle Ages and in the late nineteenth century. To your right (north) as you face the gate is a Roman tower with stone laid in the so-called 'herringbone' pattern. This distinctive detail is a feature of early Norman building and suggests that the Roman tower was repaired in the eleventh century. If you pass further around the fort in this direction, the third Roman tower has a medieval upper storey (now infilled by a machine-gun post) which was probably built as the corner tower to the Norman inner bailey to the castle. To the south of the East Gate, beyond the house which stands against the wall, are various collapsed pieces of masonry with pillboxes built within them.

HISTORY

❖

Gold coin of Carausius, showing him crowned as an emperor (286–93). He may have begun Pevensey following his declaration of independence from central Roman authority

ROMAN PEVENSEY

We know very little about the early history of Anderida, Roman Pevensey. For many years it was thought that the fort was not built until the mid-fourth century, but recent dendrochronological (tree-ring) dating of wooden piles sunk into the foundations of the walls suggest that it was actually constructed in about AD 290. At this time, the coastal defences of Roman Britain appear to have been systematically strengthened and a number of forts, such as Portchester, Burgh Castle, Richborough and Lympne, built or reconstructed. These share many architectural features with Pevensey, in particular the D-shaped wall towers which were, at this date, a novel feature of Roman military fortification.

One explanation for this sudden burst of building activity is the

Coin of Allectus, Carausius's assassin and successor (293–6)

usurpation of Britain by Carausius and Allectus between 286 and 296. Carausius rose to prominence during the reign of the emperor Diocletian as the commander of a fleet operating in the English Channel to fight piracy. In 286 he was accused of malpractice and in response proclaimed himself emperor of Britain and parts of Gaul (France) with the support of his troops. In 293 he was assassinated by a follower, Allectus, who assumed his title. After three years Allectus was also toppled from his throne, but only after a full-scale invasion of Britain. Both these men had considerable interest in fortifying the coast of Britain against the central authority in Rome and coins struck by both have been found in the foundations of Anderida's walls.

Whatever the circumstances surrounding its construction, Anderida is first documented in a late fourth-century section of the *Notitia Dignitatum,* a list of the civil and military posts in the late Roman Empire. At this time it served as one in a chain of nine forts which defended the so-called 'Saxon Shore', a coastal frontier facing attack by barbarian Saxon pirates. This chain probably extended from Portchester, Hampshire, to Brancaster on the north Norfolk coast and the individual forts within it were possibly connected by a series of watch towers.

It is not clear when the Saxon Shore forts were established as a coherent defensive system, nor exactly how they functioned militarily. All the forts are sited near anchorages or river mouths and could therefore prevent ships harbouring easily along the coast or penetrating into the interior of Britain. Some may also have had a naval capability. The *Notitia Dignitatum* actually mentions a fleet called the *Classis Anderidaensis* which presumably took its name from Anderida after being stationed here. These naval detachments probably acted in conjunction with ships based in a corresponding group of forts along the opposite coast of France. As pirate ships were funnelled together by the converging coastlines of Britain and France, the flotillas from both sides of the Channel had an increasing chance of sighting and intercepting them.

Short of the fact that Anderida was a Saxon Shore fort, nothing is known of its history until after the collapse of the Roman Empire in the west. Its walls evidently continued to shelter a British community after the withdrawal of Roman troops, and the *Anglo-Saxon Chronicle* records that in 491 it was besieged and its population slaughtered by a Saxon raiding force. After this massacre Pevensey disappears from the historical record for nearly six centuries. Although the site of the fort may have continued as a settlement during this time, it seems likely that the whole fell gradually into ruin.

Reverse of a gold medallion struck by Constantius Chlorus to celebrate his overthrow of Allectus and the restoration of central Roman authority in Britain, showing the people of London (LON) welcoming him to the city

Two of the Roman bastions in the north wall

Collapsed Roman bastion outside the twelfth-century postern gate. The sea once washed against the bottom of the bank beneath the walls.

ANGLO-NORMAN PEVENSEY

On 28 September 1066, William, Duke of Normandy, sailed his fleet, filled with an invading army, into the Bay of Pevensey. Upon landing, he immediately erected a temporary fortification to shelter his troops. He almost certainly did this within the walls of Anderida, cutting a ditch across the peninsula to isolate the ruins from the mainland and repairing the walls to create a castle. The next day his army marched away along the coast, but its subsequent victory over King Harold at the Battle of Hastings ensured the lasting importance of this rapidly erected campaign-castle at Pevensey.

The Anglo-Norman empire that William the Conqueror created after the conquest of England depended on efficient communications across the English Channel. Pevensey offered a natural anchorage facing the Normandy coast, and the castle which commanded this was of obvious strategic importance. Control of it not only ensured the lines of communication with the Continent but prevented Pevensey from being used as the base for a seaborne invasion.

After the Conquest, William left England in 1067 to make a triumphal tour of Normandy. He chose to sail from Pevensey and seems to have made a ceremonial distribution of lands there to his victorious Norman followers before a collected body of the defeated English nobility. It was possibly on this occasion that William first granted this important castle with its hinterland, known as the 'Rape' of Pevensey, into the hands of his trusted half-brother, Robert, Count of Mortain. It is probably Robert who created the first permanent defences at Pevensey, refortifying the Roman perimeter wall and creating two enclosures (or 'baileys') within its old area, divided by a ditch and timber palisade. He is also known to have founded a chapel within the castle.

After William the Conqueror's death, Pevensey's new-found strategic importance in Anglo-Norman affairs was demonstrated during the squabbles between his sons, Duke Robert of Normandy and William Rufus. In 1088, an attempt was made to install Duke Robert on the English throne in place of William Rufus. The Count of Mortain and his brother, Bishop Odo of Bayeux, supported Duke Robert and held Pevensey Castle against the king. There was a real danger that Duke Robert would invade England in the exact footsteps of the Conqueror, and to prevent this William Rufus personally supervised a siege of Pevensey by land and sea. The castle's powerful defences resisted every assault, but after six weeks a shortage of food forced the rebels to seek a truce.

❖ CATAPULT STONES ❖

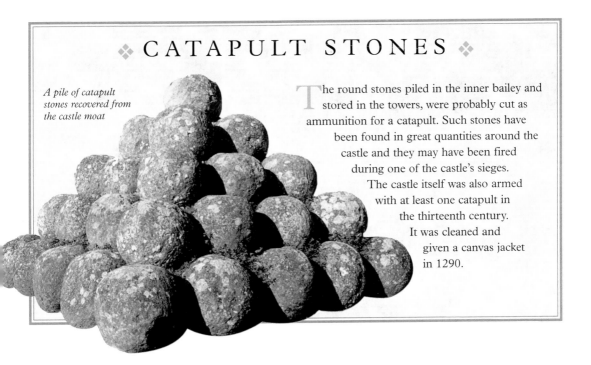

A pile of catapult stones recovered from the castle moat

The round stones piled in the inner bailey and stored in the towers, were probably cut as ammunition for a catapult. Such stones have been found in great quantities around the castle and they may have been fired during one of the castle's sieges. The castle itself was also armed with at least one catapult in the thirteenth century. It was cleaned and given a canvas jacket in 1290.

Despite this rebellion the Count of Mortain kept possession of the Rape and castle of Pevensey, but his son subsequently lost it, along with the other family estates in England, as a result of his opposition to Henry I. Henry then re-granted most of this confiscated property, including the Rape of Pevensey, to a powerful Norman lord, Gilbert Laigle. Interestingly, however, the castle appears to have been retained in royal hands as a security measure, and when Duke Robert again threatened to invade England in 1101 Henry I spent the summer at Pevensey in anticipation of an attack.

During King Stephen's reign the Laigle family lost possession of its properties. The castle was then combined again with the Rape and granted to Gilbert de Clare, Earl of Pembroke.

Shortly after receiving them Gilbert rebelled and in 1147 the castle was once more besieged by the king. One chronicler described how its most ancient walls, washed on one side by the sea, were almost inaccessible and resisted every attack. As a result, Stephen was forced to blockade the castle by sea and land and it was eventually starved into submission. After this the castle was repossessed by the Crown, in whose hands it was effectively to remain for the next eighty years.

It is in this period of royal ownership that surviving Exchequer accounts provide us with some of the earliest evidence of the castle's physical appearance. Record of repairs made to palisades in the 1180s suggest that Pevensey's defences, aside from the Roman walls, were still largely of earth and timber. Its first major stone buildings were possibly erected during the 1190s, when a series of regular and substantial payments were made towards unspecified works in the castle by Richard I. He may have constructed the existing keep and the gatehouse at this time, although the ruins of the former are thought by some to be earlier and to belong to 'the Tower of Pevensey' described in a document of 1130.

The castle Richard I developed was probably partially destroyed during the turbulent reign of his successor, John. In 1204 John lost control of Normandy, and by 1216 was desperately fighting off an invasion of England itself led by the French king's son, Prince Louis. Without the forces to garrison Pevensey he ordered that the castle be slighted. No record of this operation survives, but the fact that Pevensey played no part in the events of Louis' invasion strongly suggests that it was rendered indefensible at this date.

PEVENSEY IN THE LATER MIDDLE AGES

How and in what circumstances the castle was rebuilt is not clear, but after 1230 it passed through the hands of a sequence of royal favourites: Peter de Rivallis; Gilbert Marshal, Earl of Pembroke; and Peter of Savoy. The last of these, Peter of Savoy, was

granted the castle in 1246 and appears to have taken considerable interest in maintaining its fabric. In 1254, he arranged that the service of 'heckage' at Pevensey – a feudal obligation to maintain the timber palisades of the castle – be replaced by cash payments. The most likely explanation for this change is that he had just rendered heckage redundant

A conjectural reconstruction drawing by Philip Winton of the inner bailey of Pevensey Castle in about 1325. Note the thatch roofs of the incomplete curtain towers

by replacing the timber defences of the inner bailey with the great stone walls and towers that you see today.

Within a decade of their construction these new defences were put to the test during the baronial disturbances of Henry III's reign. On 15 May 1264, an army led by Simon de Montfort inflicted a crushing defeat on the king's forces at the Battle of Lewes. In the aftermath of the battle the royalist constable of Pevensey was ordered to surrender the castle. He refused to do so and a siege ensued. In September, local knights were called upon to help stop the garrison making destructive raids on the surrounding countryside. In addition, the besiegers dug a ditch to cut the castle off from the mainland, but this only provoked an attempt to resupply the castle with men and arms by sea in December. Ultimately the castle held out and the siege, which had cost more than £800 to conduct during its first two months alone, was eventually raised in July 1265. Some of its physical effects are also documented. In the course of the fighting, the south wall of the Roman enclosure was thrown down, and considerable damage inflicted on the neighbouring parish churches of Pevensey and Westham. These may well have been pressed into service by the attackers as siege castles.

Although the castle was handed back to Peter of Savoy after the royalist recovery at the Battle of Evesham in 1265, at his death in 1268 it passed into the hands of Henry III's queen, Eleanor of Provence; from her it descended as

❖ THE PEVENSEY BASINET ❖

The remains of three medieval helmets have been found at Pevensey Castle. This fragment is the distinctive beak-shaped visor of a helmet called a basinet which was excavated from a drain running out from under the east side of the keep. The visor is of fourteenth-century design and would originally have been attached to an open-faced headpiece. By raising and lowering it the wearer could expose or protect his face. It is punched with holes for ventilation and has slits for the eyes and mouth.

The visor from the basinet

❖ GARRISONING THE CASTLE ❖

During much of the fourteenth century the south coast of England was under threat from French raiding parties, and records survive dealing with the wages of a garrison. Throughout the period this seems to have numbered around twenty or thirty men who manned the castle in times of danger. Typically there were ten men-at-arms, twenty archers and a watchman. Provisions and armour were also provided. An account of 1370 mentions the purchase of the following provisions for the castle:

10 quarters of wheat; 4 quarters of beans; a pipe of wine; a cask of salt; 2 casks of chickpeas; 3 oxen; 20 muttons; 10 swine bought for victualling the castle; and for 8 crossbows; 9 bows; 44 sheaves of arrows bought for furnishing the castle.

Crown property, often in the possession of queens consort, for about a hundred years. In consequence of its royal ownership, a number of royal works accounts for building and repairs to the castle survive from the 1270s onwards and they present a remarkable picture of this great fortress in the high Middle Ages.

To judge from these accounts, the buildings were continually hovering on the verge of ruin despite regular and extensive repair. In 1301, for example, the main inner bailey buildings were totally reconstructed, yet only five years later they were reported to be ruinous. Limited use of the buildings was doubtless one cause of their rapid decay, but unscrupulous officials certainly played their part too. The then constable, Roger de Levelande, was accused of breaking up and selling the great wooden bridge to the castle

and some 'wardens' of burning the timber of a disused barn. In 1306, it was estimated that these and other damages and dilapidations would cost over £1000 to repair. Aside from the documented repairs, considerable undocumented work must also have gone on. In particular, archaeological excavation has shown that the keep was partially demolished and rebuilt in about 1325.

In 1372, the castle passed into the possession of John of Gaunt, Duke of Lancaster. He came into conflict with Richard II's government during the king's minority and pointedly refused to garrison Pevensey against French attacks during 1377, claiming that if it were destroyed he had enough money to rebuild it. Such actions fuelled the Duke's unpopularity and in 1381, during the Peasants' Revolt, a mob burnt the castle's court rolls and abused his steward.

❖ THE 1399 SIEGE OF PEVENSEY ❖

In 1394 John of Gaunt appointed Sir John Pelham to the Constableship of Pevensey Castle. This family retainer later supported Gaunt's banished son, Henry Bolingbroke, when he returned from exile to claim his inheritance in 1399. Famously, Bolingbroke went on to usurp the throne from Richard II. When Bolingbroke first landed Pelham was besieged in the castle by local levies. He wrote a celebrated letter to Bolingbroke informing him of his circumstances. The letter was once wrongly thought to have been written by his wife.

'My dear Lord ... if it please you to know of my affairs, I am here by laid in manner of a siege, with the counties of Sussex, Surrey and a great part of Kent, so that I may not out, nor no vitals get me without much difficulty. Wherefore my dear may it please you, by the advice of your wise council, to give remedy to the salvation of your castle, and withstand the malice of the shires ... Farewell my dere Lord, the Holy Trinity keep you from your enemies, and soon send me good tidings of you. Written at Pevensey in the Castle, on Saint Jacob day last past. By your own poor, J. Pelham.'

When Bolingbroke was crowned as Henry IV Pelham received the Castle and Honour of Pevensey in recompense for his services.

A medieval siege assault, from a 14th-century manuscript illustration. Notice the catapult, and the defending crossbowman.

Pemfey in Suffex

Detail of a mid-17th-century engraving of the castle by Wenceslaus Hollar – the earliest known view of Pevensey. In the centre, behind the gatehouse, are the ruins of the keep

THE DECLINE OF THE CASTLE

The siege of 1399 was the last that Pevensey Castle faced. During the fifteenth century the castle continued to be maintained and repaired and served as a state prison. Among those held here were King James I of Scotland and Joan of Navarre, the second wife of Henry IV, imprisoned by her stepson, Henry V. Under the Tudors the castle fell out of use altogether, and a survey of 1573 records that the buildings were in total ruin. The defences were entirely neglected until the threat of the Spanish Armada caused the construction of a gun emplacement, armed with two cannons described as 'demi-culverins of small value'. One of these cannons still survives on a modern reproduction carriage in the inner bailey.

Queen Joan of Navarre, Henry IV's second wife, from the effigy on her tomb in Canterbury Cathedral. In 1419 she was accused by her stepson, Henry V, of plotting his death by witchcraft and was imprisoned. She was released in 1422

Pillboxes built into the ruins of the keep during the Second World War. They are constructed from flint to make them blend in with the Roman and medieval fabric

THE SECOND WORLD WAR DEFENCES

Between the sixteenth and the twentieth century Pevensey Castle played no part in major national events, and its buildings were left to decay. It was presented to the State in 1925 by the Duke of Devonshire but, having been repaired as a historic monument, the events of the Second World War gave a strange twist to its history. After the fall of France in the summer of 1940, Pevensey once more became a potential landing-place for an invasion. A command and observation post was set up in the castle and the perimeter defences were refortified: pillboxes for machine-gun posts were built and a blockhouse for anti-tank weapons constructed in the mouth of the Roman West Gate. The towers of the inner bailey were refitted internally to create barracks for its garrison, which included Home Guard, British, Canadian and US Army Air Corps units. In order to make the new work blend in with the old, and also to provide camouflage, these alterations were made under the supervision of the Ministry of Works, the government department responsible for the fabric. The castle was returned to their control in 1945 and the decision was taken to leave most of the recently constructed military installations in place as evidence of an important recent phase in the castle's history.

FURTHER READING

Rudyard Kipling, *Puck of Pook's Hill*.

M. Fulford and I. Tyers, 'The date of Pevensey and the defence of an *"Imperium Britanniarum"'*, *Antiquity*, lxix (1995).

J. Goodall, *The English Castle*, 2011.

S. Johnson, *The Roman Forts of the Saxon Shore*, 1976.

C. Peers, 'Pevensey Castle', *Sussex Archaeological Collections*, lxxiv (1983).

L.F. Salzmann, 'Documents relating to Pevensey Castle', *Sussex Archaeological Collections*, xlix (1906).

K. Thompson, 'Lords, castellans, constables and dowagers: the Rape of Pevensey from the 11th to 13th century', *Sussex Archaeological Collections*, cxxxv (1997).

S.K. Walker, 'Letters to the Dukes of Lancaster in 1381 and 1399', *English Historical Review*, cvi (1991).